Bristol Channel Shipping

Remembered

Sunshine and shadows in a safe haven. The Finnish steamship, *Teti N*, in the Queen Alexandra Dock, Cardiff.

Bristol Channel
Shipping

Remembered

Chris Collard

The
History
Press

First published in 2002 by Tempus Publishing

Reprinted in 2010 by
The History Press
The Mill, Brimscombe Port,
Stroud, Gloucestershire, GL5 2QG
www.thehistorypress.co.uk

ISBN 978 0 7524 2388 3

Typesetting and origination by
Tempus Publishing Limited
Printed and bound in England

'Oh, where are you going to, all you Big Steamers,
With England's own coal, up and down the salt seas?'
'We are going to fetch you your bread and your butter,
Your beef, pork, and mutton, eggs, apples, and cheese.'

Big Steamers, Rudyard Kipling (1865-1936).

The Hadley Shipping Co.'s oil tanker *Cerinthus*, of 1954, entering Barry Docks in April 1962.

Contents

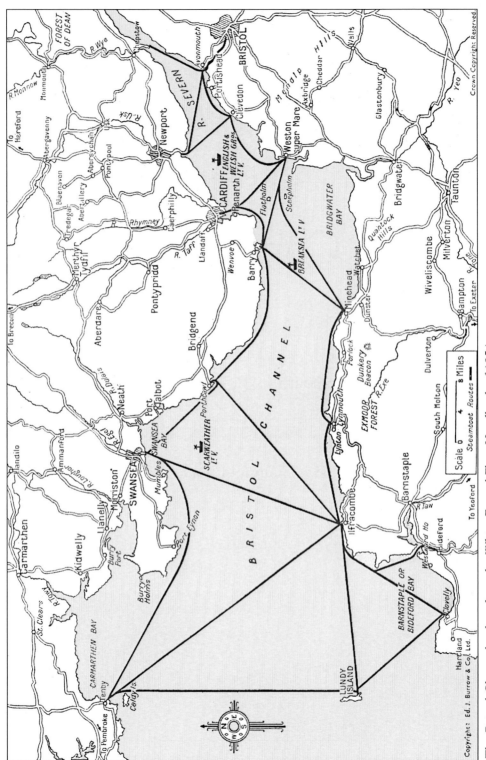

The Bristol Channel, taken from the White Funnel Fleet Handbook of 1954.

Introduction

The Bristol Channel is a dangerous waterway. It is open to the fury of the storms which sweep in from the Atlantic Ocean; the rise and fall of its tides, and the speed of its tidal flows, are among the greatest in the world; rocks, mudflats and sandbanks abound. It is an area of great contrasts; its shores range from the rugged grandeur of the north Devon cliffs to the vast, flat sandy beaches of Swansea Bay – both of which, in their different ways, are equally dangerous to shipping.

Nevertheless, its navigational hazards did not deter the development of the wide variety of its ports from diminutive harbours to major dock complexes. Such diverse ports bred a similar diversity of vessels which used them, and was also reflected in the cargoes they carried. With the development of railway and road transport, as their branches radiated countrywide, so the Bristol Channel ports assumed even greater importance as they drew lucrative business from ever widening commercial territory.

In its heyday the Bristol Channel was a thriving estuary where ships of all descriptions were to be seen, ranging from the elegant passenger and cargo liners to the utilitarian tugs and dredgers, each one fulfilling its own essential function in pursuit of the continuing flow of commerce. The post-war years, however, brought about a slow but steady decline, which accelerated during the 1960s and has left the Channel a mere shadow of its former self.

The 1960s were a period of great change for the Bristol Channel's excursion vessels. Since 1887 the paddle steamers of P&A Campbell's White Funnel Fleet were a regular summer sight, busily carrying passengers to and from the ports and resorts of the channel's English and Welsh coasts; but the old order was changing. The expensive-to-run paddle steamers no longer paid their way and were replaced by the more economical but less charismatic motor vessels.

During the post-war era ships in general were changing. Many 'old timers' were still to be seen, belching smoke from their tall funnels, but motor vessels were gradually replacing them. Although they were often larger ships than their coal burning counterparts, smaller crews sufficed. They were much cleaner ships, of greater speed, requiring less maintenance and quicker and cheaper refuelling. The old steamships were, however, the maritime 'characters', although I wonder how much this meant to their crews, living in their spartan accommodation with its lack of 'mod cons'.

During the early years of my childhood in the 1950s, my grandfather, then a coal trimmer in Newport Docks, would take me, on the crossbar of his bicycle, to see the ships on which he worked. He, and my father, would often take me for trips aboard the White Funnel steamers, from which the constant flow of shipping could be seen at close quarters. And what a pageant of ships were to be seen, even in the years of decline.

Fortunately, during those last great years, my love of ships coincided with an enthusiasm for photography and resulted in a large collection of negatives. Few of them were printed at the time as they represented ordinary, everyday scenes which I felt would be there forever. How wrong I was!

This book takes us on a nostalgic, circular tour from Bristol, down the channel to its westerly limits and then eastward along the coast of South Wales to Newport, and shows some of those once familiar scenes, now just memories of this great waterway.

One

Bristol and Avonmouth

Above: A view from the end of St Augustine's Reach, looking towards the City Centre, with barges laden with wood pulp in the foreground. The Floating Harbour was constructed between 1804 and 1809, and, at a cost of £600,000, provided Bristol with a tide-free dock. It was a considerable feat of civil engineering, its construction entailing the diverting of the river and the placing of locks at each end of its former course. Much of the digging for the diversion, known as the New Cut, was carried out by French prisoners of the Napoleonic wars.

Previous page: Bristol – 'The Metropolis of the West' – has been an important maritime centre since the Middle Ages. It is situated in the counties of Gloucestershire and Somerset but is independent of both, enjoying the distinction of being a county in itself, having been so created by special charter of Edward III in recompense for the great services rendered to him by the shipping of the port.

St Augustine's Reach, which had formed part of the city's dock system since the early thirteenth century, brought ships right into the heart of Bristol. In this 1966 view, the statues of Edward Colston, the philanthropist (in the foreground), and Edmund Burke (to its right), said to have been the city's greatest parliamentary representative, overlook, not only the bustling activity of the City Centre, but also the cranes of the Floating Harbour in the distance. For many years the waterway extended even further into the centre and was crossed by St Augustines Bridge, formerly situated close to the statues. Sugar, wine, rum and tobacco were just some of the many commodities which combined to make Bristol one of the world's greatest ports in past centuries.

The General Steam Navigation Co.'s steamship *Crane*, unloading her cargo in St Augustine's Reach. The GSN maintained a large fleet of cargo vessels, ranging from 200 to 2,000 gross tons, which operated a complex network of short sea services from the UK to European and Scandanavian ports.

The Swedish steamship, *Sonja*, unloads her cargo of wood pulp from Scandanavia in St Augustines Reach.

Above and below: The *Medway*, one of the many small steam tugs which were frequently to be seen bustling about the Floating Harbour.

A quiet backwater of the Floating Harbour on a Sunday evening in 1964.

The Floating Harbour was the winter home of the P&A Campbell White Funnel Fleet of paddle steamers from the late 1880s until 1956. In this 1914 view, six white funnels can be seen in addition to the *Brighton* (the two-funnelled vessel towards the left), owned by Pockett's of Swansea, and the Bideford-registered ketch, *Susanna*, on the right.

The *Britannia*, flagship of the White Funnel Fleet from 1896 to 1946, turning in the River Avon in the early 1900s. On the left can be seen the locks which lead into the Cumberland Basin and the Floating Harbour. On the right is the New Cut.

The *Bristol Queen* replaced the *Britannia* as flagship of the White Funnel Fleet on entering service in September 1946. She is seen here approaching Hotwells Landing Stage in 1964.

One of the Bristol Steam Navigation Co's vessels, the *Pluto*, of 1950, approaches the Cumberland Basin locks in the summer of 1966. At that time she, and several other members of the company's fleet of seven vessels, ran a weekly cargo service from Bristol to Belgium and Holland.

Above: The spectacular Clifton Suspension Bridge. In 1753 a Bristol wine merchant left £1,000 in investment stipulating that on its increase to £10,000 it should be used to finance the construction of a stone bridge across the Avon Gorge. In 1830, when the investment had reached the figure of £10,000, engineers were invited to compete for the project. The design accepted was that of Isambard Kingdom Brunel. In 1836 work began but ceased in 1843 after £45,000 had been spent. The project was re-commenced in 1861. Sadly, Brunel was not destined to see the outcome of his venture. The bridge was opened on 8 December 1864, five years after his death. The distance from pier to pier was 702ft and its height from the riverbed was 290ft. The total cost from its commencement was £100,000.

Previous page:
Above: The tug, *Shaftesbury*, tows a string of barges, bound for Avonmouth Docks, past Hotwells Landing Stage. On the left can be seen the remains of the entrance to the 500ft long, hydraulic, Clifton Rocks railway, opened in 1893, which connected Clifton with the hot well pump, situated close to the railway's lower terminus. Clifton, with its wealth of elegant houses built above the Avon Gorge for the merchants and shipowners when the city's fortunes were at their peak, became a fashionable spa in the eighteenth century. The nobility came from far and wide to drink the waters of the hot well. It was finally closed having been contaminated with river water.

Below: The *Shaftesbury* proceeds down river towards the Clifton Suspension Bridge.

Above: The Dutch coaster, *Lonelil*, making her way up river on a hazy morning in 1964. Many Dutch and German shipowners managed additional vessels on behalf of smaller concerns or individual 'captains/owners'. Frequently the ships were crewed by the families of their masters; a homely touch often being provided by their wives, who adorned the bridges with plants and flowers.

Previous page:
Above: The Port of Bristol Authority's Sea Mills signal station. In the upstairs room the lookout can be seen. He would be on duty over the high water period to relay information on the shipping movements in the river to each vessel that passed, by means of a microphone and loudspeakers. Another such station was situated farther down the river at Shirehampton.

Below: The Dutch coaster, *Adine*, has just passed the Bristol suburb of Sea Mills, where, over 2,000 years ago Roman galleys used to ride at anchor in the entrance to the River Trym, one of the Avon's tributaries. The entrance to the Trym is crossed by the bridge, just visible behind the stern of the *Adine*.

The *Paul* M approaching Sea Mills on her journey up stream. She was one of the many coasters owned by Thomas J. Metcalf, all of which were given male or female christian names, with the suffix M.

The William Sloan coaster, *Deveron*, of 1938, makes her way up the River Avon. She was sold to Greece in November 1963 and renamed *Nissos Delos*.

One of the Port of Bristol Authority's dredgers, *B D Clifton*, (BD denoting Bristol Docks), heads down river to discharge her 'cargo' of River Avon mud into the channel.

The coaster, *Mountstewart*, of the Belfast, Mersey & Manchester Shipping Co., in Sea Mills Reach.

The Dutch coaster, *Mascotte*, seen from the Shirehampton Signal Station, passes the village of Pill.

The Dutch coaster *Olivier van Noort* passes Avonmouth Docks on her way to Bristol.

The Dutch coaster, *Valbella*, has just left the mouth of the River Avon and heads out to sea.

Above: Avonmouth's passenger trade had dwindled by the 1930s, but for some years during the 1960s the Swedish-America Line scheduled visits to the Bristol Channel as part of its 'Springtime Cruises'. Here the 21,141 gross tons motor vessel *Kungsholm*, of 1953, lies at anchor in Walton Bay, near Clevedon, in 1964. The White Funnel steamers were used as tenders and took the passengers to Avonmouth, where coaches waited to take them on tours of local places of interest.

Previous page: The Metcalf motor coaster, *Eileen M*, heading seaward past Avonmouth Docks.

Opposite: The entrance to Avonmouth Docks. The tortuous passage up the River Avon precluded larger ships entering the Bristol City Docks. Avonmouth, however, with its deep water approaches held no such restrictions. Passenger liners and the largest cargo vessels became frequent visitors. The original dock was opened in 1877. The larger Royal Edward Dock was opened on 9 July 1908 by King Edward VII and Queen Alexandra, and was extended in 1928 with the opening of the Eastern Arm. Extensive cold stores, granaries, fruit stores and oil storage tanks brought a wide variety of cargoes and ships from all over the world.

A Dutch coaster enters the locks at Avonmouth while the P&A Campbell motor vessel, *Westward Ho*, leaves the south pier having discharged passengers from the Swedish America liner, *Gripsholm*, in 1966.

The Bristol pilot cutter, *George Ray*, leaving Avonnmouth Dock. She was built by J.I. Thornycroft at Southampton and entered service in early 1962.

With Avonmouth's oil storage tanks in the background, an unidentified tanker awaits the tide to enter the dock.

The Swedish tanker, *Zelos*, heads out to sea from Avonmouth. The flag flying from her mainmast, half white, half red, indicates that she has a pilot aboard.

The Dutch oil tanker *Bussum* heading down channel from Avonmouth.

The Donaldson Line cargo vessel, *Letitia*, at anchor in the deep water of Kingroad, off Portishead, in 1963. She was a regular visitor to the Bristol Channel ports, sailing to Montreal in summer, and St Johns, Newfoundland, during the winter.

The German owned *Clare Hugo Stinnes*, with a deck cargo of timber, awaits the tide off Avonmouth in 1963.

A veteran coastal tanker of the Esso fleet, *Allegheny*, built in 1921, passes Portishead in September 1960.

The diminutive coaster, *Abbots Leigh*, owned by F. Ashmead of Bristol, making her way down channel off Clevedon.

Two

Down Channel

Above: The North Devon coast, from Porlock Bay to Bull Point, is unrivalled in the grandeur of its cliff scenery. A short distance west of the Somerset/Devon border, the Foreland Point light-house stands 220ft above sea level. The White Funnel steamers, on their way to Lynmouth and Ilfracombe, frequently passed close to the point and their masters usually blew a long blast on the ship's whistle as a greeting to the resident lighthouse keepers and their families. This would often bring the children running to the wall to return the greeting with their waving handkerchiefs.

Previous page: Flat Holm seen from the paddle steamer *Cardiff Queen* on a crossing from Cardiff to Weston during a westerly gale on Wednesday 16 September 1964.

At the approach to the upper reaches of the Bristol Channel stand the islands of Flat and Steep Holm. 'Holm' was the ancient Norse word for 'island' and is a legacy of the Danish invasion of the tenth century. Flat Holm, which, under an ancient charter, falls within the water boundaries of the parish of St Stephen, Bristol, is one and a half miles in circumference and covers an area of about sixty acres, much of which provides good pasturage for sheep. The island's colourful history embraces such diversities as a medieval ecclesiastical presence, military activity from 1860 to the Second World War, and Cardiff's cholera isolation hospital. Bristol's Merchant Venturers built the first lighthouse in 1738 which consisted of an open fire in a brazier on top of the tower. Trinity House installed an oil lantern in 1820 which was replaced by the present lantern in 1866. Its foghorn, once the loudest in the channel, is now silent; modern navigational aids having made it redundant.

In the shelter of one of the valleys of the North Devon coast lies the town of Ilfracombe. Once a secluded fishing village; the arrival of the railway and excursion steamer services transformed it into a fashionable resort. This view of the *Bristol Queen* at the pier on 20 May 1961 resembles, in many respects, that seen through Victorian eyes. Construction of the pier began in 1870 and was completed in 1873 under the auspicies of the Lord of the Manor, Sir Bourchier Palk Wrey. The fourteenth-century chapel of St Nicholas, the Patron Saint of Sailors, which overlooks the pier from Lantern Hill, was once a dwelling occupied by a husband and wife and their fourteen children! On the left is the inner harbour, protected by the old stone pier. The Ilfracombe life-boatmen justly claim an outstanding service record. The lifeboat was towed by tractor, from the boathouse at the base of Lantern Hill, through the narrow streets to the harbour, from where it was launched.

On seeing Ilfracombe in such calm weather, it is difficult to imagine the ferocity of the winter storms, which send huge seas sweeping into the harbour. Such a storm was raging through the Bristol Channel on Sunday 13 November 1949, when the Spanish steamer, *Monte Gurugu*, outward bound from Newport to Genoa fully laden with coal, lost her rudder and began to ship water in overwhelming seas between Lundy and Hartland Point. A combined operation by the Ilfracombe, Appledore and Clovelly lifeboats saved twenty-four of her crew of thirty-seven, and recovered five bodies. For their outstanding rescue, in conditions said to have been the worst for many years, the three coxswains and their crews were presented with awards by both the Royal National Lifeboat Institution and the Spanish Naval Attaché, on behalf of the Spanish Lifeboat Society, at a ceremony held on the pier on 30 June 1950.

Above and below: The *Westward Ho* arriving at Ilfracombe in 1966, showing that even a moderate swell caused ships to roll heavily on their approach to the pier. The *Westward Ho* was launched as the *Vecta* at the yard of J.I. Thornycroft of Southampton in 1938, for the Red Funnel Company. She ran a regular service between Southampton and Cowes, carrying up to fifteen cars as well as passengers, in addition to running a variety of cruises. She was purchased by P&A Campbell Ltd in September 1965 and ran in the Bristol Channel until serious engine trouble laid her up in 1971. She later became a floating restaurant in Manchester's docklands.

The *Cardiff Queen* at Ilfracombe pier in 1961. The *Cardiff Queen* was built by Fairfield's of Govan in 1947 – the younger sister of the P&A Campbell flagship *Bristol Queen*. She sailed on the south coast during the 1952 and 1953 seasons but was otherwise employed in the Bristol Channel. She was a familiar sight at all the channel resorts but for five years operated the Swansea to Ilfracombe service – notorious for its rough passages.

The *Westward Ho* at Ilfracombe pier in the 1970s. In the foreground is the *Elizabeth*, a former local fishing vessel which was converted for passenger carrying and became known to many holiday-makers for her short cruises along the North Devon coast.

The motor vessel *Balmoral* leaving Ilfracombe in the early 1970s. The *Balmoral*, following in the footsteps of the *Vecta/Westward Ho*, dates from 1949 when she was launched for the Red Funnel Co. of Southampton. She also ran a regular car and passenger carrying service to the Isle of Wight until purchased by P&A Campbell Ltd in 1969. On the demise of Campbells she went to Dundee, where an abortive attempt was made to use her as a floating restaurant. She returned to the Bristol Channel in 1986 as consort to the paddle steamer *Waverley*.

The village of Appledore, with the lifeboat at its moorings. A few miles west of Ilfracombe stands Bull Point, and the start of the semicircular sweep of Bideford, or Barnstaple Bay. Halfway around the bay, situated at the junction of the Taw and Torridge estuaries, is Appledore. The village has a long history of shipbuilding and when this photograph was taken, in 1963, was turning out many fine vessels from its large, covered dry dock.

About a mile offshore is the treacherous sandbank known as Bideford Bar. The sixteenth-century traveller and chronicler, John Leland, wrote of the estuary, 'The Haven entery is barrid with sande and the enterie into it is daungerous'. A masterpiece of understatement! Innumerable shipwrecks and much loss of life over the years led to the stationing of a lifeboat at Appledore in the early nineteenth century.

Bideford Quay in August 1963. A short distance up the River Torridge lies the town of Bideford. Its picturesque quay was built in the seventeenth century when the port's overseas trade was at its height. Wool was being imported from Spain and Ireland for the local textile mills and the woven cloth was then exported. The major imports of salted cod from Newfoundland and tobacco from America declined in the late eighteenth century and, although the quay was frequently used by commercial shipping until the 1960s, trade then dwindled and fishing boats became predominant.

Having unloaded her cargo at one of Barnstaple's riverside quays, the Thomas J. Metcalf motor coaster, *Michael* M, leaves the Tawe/Torridge estuary with the cutter in attendance, waiting to 'pick out' the pilot after seeing the ship safely across Bideford Bar.

The Bristol City Line's cargo vessel, *Coventry City*, returns from her maiden voyage from Avonmouth to Canada and is seen crossing Bideford Bay in September 1966.

Clovelly from the sea in August 1965. About six miles east of Hartland Point, on the southern shore of Bideford Bay, lies the hillside village of Clovelly, with its cobbled streets, picturesque harbour and ancient granite quay. Clovelly was never a 'commercial' port but a fishing village, although the produce of the neighbourhood, as well as incoming goods were shipped through its harbour. The village possesses a fine maritime heritage; its lifeboatmen frequently had to put to sea in appalling weather to effect remarkable rescues on this most perilous of coastlines.

At the north-western extremity of Devon stands Hartland Point. Ptolemy's 'Promontory of Hercules' is surrounded by the grandeur of the wild cliffs on the landward side, and a turbulent tidal race, the Hartland Overfalls, to seaward. The wise mariner steers well clear of Hartland Point! On a plateau below the headland, 120ft above sea level stands the lighthouse, and on the horizon, the island of Lundy.

Previous page: Lundy Island, three miles long and half a mile wide, marks the westerly limit of the Bristol Channel, 10½ miles NNW of Hartland Point. Nearly 400ft high, this granite rock, volcanic in origin, acts as a breakwater during the prevailing westerly gales, and many ships shelter in Lundy Roads, off the island's east coast. The Elder Bretheren of Trinity House, the body which provides and maintains the beacons around the English and Welsh coasts, first landed here in 1819 and built the stone lighthouse, which replaced the timber structure erected by the Merchant Venturers of Bristol. The new light was considerably more powerful than its predecessor, but its height, and the fact that it had been built on the summit of the island, meant that the lantern was frequently obscured by low cloud. It was abandoned in 1897 on completion of the north and south lighthouses.

Below: Lundy's north lighthouse. At a height of 165ft above mean high water, in comparison with the 538ft of the old light, its beam was much less susceptible to obscurity by low cloud.

Lundy's south lighthouse, built 175ft above the mean high water level, on the promontory of Lametor, with Rat Island on the extreme left, the gap in between being known as Hell's Gates! At the bottom right can be seen the path which leads to the landing beach, with its wheeled landing stage, complete with small tractor which moved it up or down the shingle beach according to the state of the tide.

Above: In the early 1960s P&A Campbell Ltd revived one of its occasional pre-war trips when the *Bristol Queen* crossed the channel from Ilfracombe to Milford Haven. The pilot is seen boarding the paddle steamer to take her into the dock entrance.

The large expanse of Milford Haven's natural harbour has seen a wide variety of vessels through the ages – whalers, trawlers, coasters, sailing warships and, in the 1960s, because of its deep water – supertankers. In the winter of 1956 Milford Haven was stated to be 'The Port of the Future' when the Esso Petroleum Co. announced its plans for the construction of an oil refinery. The first cargo of crude oil was pumped ashore at the Esso terminal on 8 July 1960 from the tanker, *Esso Portsmouth*, and the terminal building was officially opened on 3 November 1960 by the Duke of Edinburgh.

In August 1957 work began on the British Petroleum Co.'s terminal, after Royal Assent had been obtained for its construction and the laying of a sixty-mile overland pipeline to its refinery at Llandarcy, Swansea. BP's terminal, in Angle Bay, received its first cargo of 39,000 tons of crude oil for Llandarcy from the tanker, *British Statesman*, at the end of August 1960. The Gulf Oil Co.'s terminal was opened in the summer of 1964, and the Regent oil terminal was opened on 26 October 1964, at which the Cunard liner, *Mauretania* was present, carrying company officials and guests.

Previous page: A blast on the whistle of the *Cardiff Queen* echoes around the cliffs of Lundy as her master, Capt. Phillip Power, warns passengers of impending departure, on Tuesday 11 June 1963. On the right is the *Lundy Gannet*, the regular Lundy packet which carried passengers and supplies between the island and Bideford Quay. She was built in 1949 as the *Pride of Bridlington*, for trawling in the North Sea, and retained her Hull registration number – H57 – throughout her Bristol Channel career. Her Lundy service began in June 1956 and lasted for nearly twenty years, crossing once or twice per week and thrice weekly during the summer months.

The Esso tanker, *Esso Winchester*, cautiously makes her way up Milford Haven towards the Esso refinery on 28 July 1963.

The Norwegian tanker, *Polyana*, at Milford Haven on 28 July 1963. The picturesque surroundings of the Haven were in marked contrast to the, then, futuristic pipelines and storage tanks of the refineries.

The ocean-going salvage tug, *Turmoil*, at Milford Haven, 28 July 1963. She was on a long-term charter from the Admiralty to the Overseas Towage & Salvage Co. Ltd of Milford Haven. She had been built in 1945 and her diesel engines could generate 3,000bhp – considerably more than the average tug's 500-1,000bhp. The *Turmoil* had featured prominently in the news in 1952 when she towed the stricken Norwegian cargo vessel *Flying Enterprise* through heavy seas in the English Channel towards Falmouth. Her master, Capt. Henrik Carlsen, remained alone on his ship, which, despite the efforts of the *Turmoil*, sank in the storm-tossed waters when only fifty miles from the Cornish coast.

The Swansea pilot cutter *Seamark* and the White Funnel motor vessel *Balmoral* at Pockett's Wharf on the River Tawe, Swansea, in 1969.

Before the Industrial Revolution Swansea was a small harbour and fishing village at the mouth of the River Tawe. Towards the end of the eighteenth century, the increasing world-wide demand for copper led to the establishment of smelting works on the river above the town. Copper ore was imported from South America, many of the ships sailing around Cape Horn. Zinc and tinplate works joined the smelters and, along with coal and general cargo, exports reached phenomenal levels. The harbour was expanded with new docks and by the middle of the nineteenth century more than 10,000 ships sailed in and out of the port each year.

The Queens Dock, Swansea, was opened in 1920 for the importing of crude oil and the exporting of refined products. National Oil Refineries Ltd, allied with the Anglo Persian Oil Co. occupied a large area of land laid out with refineries, storage tanks and pipe lines. Extensive facilities were provided for bunkering even the largest of vessels.

Sunset over the Queens Dock, with Mumbles Head just visible in the background. The solitary occupant of the dock is one of the ships of the Lowland Tanker Co. Ltd, a subsidiary of British Petroleum.

The 8,775 gross ton BP tanker, *British General*, of 1950, in the Queens Dock in 1963. At that time BP and its subsidiary companies were operating a fleet of over 150 oil tankers.

Dutch seamen at the stern of the Holland America Line's, *Alblasserdyk*, berthing at Swansea in 1963.

The *Alblasserdyk*, safely moored in the Kings Dock.

One of the Elder Dempster Line's cargo vessels, the *Owerri*, in the Kings Dock, in 1963.

A German cargo vessel in the Prince of Wales Dock, Swansea, in 1963.

A lightvessel undergoing maintenance at the Trinity House Depot in the Kings Dock, Swansea, in 1963.

The Trinity House tender, *Alert*, in the King's Dock, Swansea, in 1963.

The former Mersey based tug, *Caswell*, in the Kings Dock, Swansea. She was one of the large fleet of tugs owned by the Alexandra Towing Co. and was sold to Haulbowline Industries of Cork for breaking up in March 1969.

Left to right: The tugs *Langland*, of 1916, *Caswell* and *Murton*, await their next turn of duty in a corner of the Kings Dock.

The *Brynforth* and *Sloyne* in the Prince of Wales Dock, Swansea, in 1961. The *Brynforth* was the former Clyde tug *Flying Hurricane*, acquired by the Britannia Towing Co. of Swansea in 1956. She had been built originally for the Admiralty at Wallsend, on the Tyne, as the *Empire Thistle* and was broken up at Silloth, on the Solway Firth, in August 1965.

The British Transport Commission's bucket dredger, *Abertawe*, at Swansea in 1963.

With a naval pinnace as her deck cargo, the Royal Fleet Auxiliary, *Robert Middleton*, makes her way up channel, across Swansea Bay.

A hazy summer's day at Mumbles in 1963, with the *Bristol Queen* approaching the pier after a cruise along the Gower Coast. The building of the lifeboat house, an offshoot of the pier, began in 1913 but was interrupted by the First World War. The slipway had been completed by 1916 but it was not until 1922 that the boathouse was erected.

Although occuring outside the period of this book, no mention of Mumbles can be made without reference to the lifeboat's involvement in one of the Bristol Channel's greatest tragedies.

On the afternoon of Wednesday 23 April 1947, the 7,219gt liberty ship, *Samtampa*, bound from Middlesbrough, in ballast, for one of the Newport dry docks, steamed up the Bristol Channel before gale force winds. She was experiencing engine trouble and dropped both of her anchors in Swansea Bay. By 4.50 p.m. both the port and starboard cables had parted, owing to the heavy seas, and within twenty minutes she had been driven across the bay and broadside on to the rocky ledges of Sker Point, near Porthcawl. The exceptionally heavy seas caused her to break up and by 8 p.m. she had become a total wreck. Rockets were fired from the shore but were ineffectual against the force of the 80mph winds. The Mumbles lifeboat had been called out at 6.10 p.m. and set off across Swansea Bay. Shortly afterwards, radio contact was lost. On the following morning the *Samtampa* was found to have broken into three parts and the lifeboat was found, upturned on the rocks some distance away.

On the morning of Thursday 24 April 1947 a rescue team carries away a body from the wreck of the *Samtampa* to a temporary mortuary in the sand dunes of Sker Point.

The bridge and engine room section of the wreck.

The bow and stern sections 200 yards apart. The thirty-nine crew members of the *Samtampa* perished.

The upturned wreck of the Mumbles lifeboat, *Edward, Prince of Wales*. Her crew of eight were lost, it is believed, when an exceptional sea turned her over and drove her across the rocks.

One of the coastal tankers of the John Harker fleet passes Nash Point on her way westward along the Welsh coast. The two lighthouses, and the fog signal station in between, were built on Nash Point in 1832. One displayed a low level and the other a high level light; when these were aligned the mariner knew that he should take evasive action to avoid grounding on the Nash Sands – the extensive sandbank running from the point, westward towards Swansea Bay. As navigational aids became more sophistcated, the low level light was discontinued, its lantern having been removed by the late 1960s.

Another of the Harker fleet, *Waterdale H*, fully laden, makes her way up the Welsh coast near Barry.

The *Corbrae*, one of the Cardiff owned vessels of John Cory & Sons Ltd, at anchor near the Merkur buoy, off Barry. The buoy marks the position of the wreck of the 4,000gt Finnish steamer *Merkur*, which sank after a collision on 9 May 1920. The Cory ships were often known as the 'black diamond boats' because of the funnel emblem.

Three

Barry and the Bristol Channel Pilots

Above: The tug *Windsor* guiding the Liberian tanker *Sol* towards the Lady Windsor lock. The *Sol*, built in 1949, after a period laid up in Barry, was sold to Greek buyers in November 1964 and renamed *Kava Maleas*.

Previous page: The Liberian tanker *Sol* entering Barry Dock in 1962.

Congestion at Cardiff Docks and the consequent delays in shipping coal were becoming acute in the late nineteenth century. Many vessels spent days riding idly at anchor in the roads and the docks themselves were so full of ships that it was possible to cross from one side to the other by walking across their decks.

In the early 1880s, when the first Barry Dock was planned, there were only about seventeen inhabited houses in the 'village', and its approximately eighty inhabitants were dependent chiefly on agriculture.

In the late nineteenth century Barry Island was was joined to the mainland by a causeway, and this provided shelter for a new set of docks and coal sidings. Among the engineers who supervised their construction was H.M. Brunel, the younger son of Isambard Kingdom.

The population of the town had increased to about 13,000 when the £2 million dock was opened on 19 September 1889. It covered 73 acres and was, at that time, the largest in the world. Subsequently two further docks were built and the total deep water area became 114 acres.

4,000 ships per year berthed at Barry during the boom years and in the record year, 1913, of the 37 million tons of coal exported from the South Wales ports, 11 million were shipped through Barry.

The tug *Windsor*, built in Bristol in 1932 and broken up at Cashmore's yard, Newport, in March 1965.

Astern of the *Sol*, the *Tregarth*, formerly the Milford Haven tug, *Neylandia*, assists with her docking.

The tug *Emphatic* at Barry in June 1960. She was built at Selby for the Admiralty in 1943 as the *Empire Joan*, and was purchased by Edmund Hancock Ltd, for service at Barry from August 1958.

An unidentified ship of the massive merchant fleet of the former USSR leaving Barry in April 1962.

The London & Rochester Shipping Co.'s coaster, *Kindrence*, leaving Barry in April 1962, with a cargo of coal for the Yelland power station on the River Taw.

The Cardiff pilot cutter *Lady Merrett* at Barry in May 1962. This vessel replaced the *Lady Seager*, of 1919, the last of the Bristol Channel steam pilot cutters, on 6 April 1960.

Shortly before a violent thunderstorm in May 1962, the *Lady Merrett* leaves Barry harbour to put a pilot aboard an inward bound ship. The veteran tramp steamer offshore is the *Kylequeen*.

The *Cardiff Queen* at Barry Pier in April 1962. The Bristol pilot cutter *George Ray* is moored alongside her port quarter.

The Barry pilot cutter *Quest* leaving the harbour in May 1962.

The Newport pilot cutter *Alpha II* in Barry harbour, May 1962.

On Monday 1 January that year, I began my apprenticeship with the Newport Pilotage Authority. The authority's pilot cutters were the *Spencer*, built by J. Tyrell at Arklow, which began service in December 1959, and the *Alpha II*, named after a former sailing cutter, also built by J. Tyrell, which had begun service early in 1958. Both vessels were approximately 55ft in length and had a maximum speed of 10 knots. Like all of the up-channel pilot cutters they were based at Barry. The Newport pilots and the nine apprentices, four senior and five junior, were housed in the converted and extended Barry Pier railway station building. My first morning was spent with one of the senior boys in learning the basics of the pilot cutter and my duties. That afternoon I went out to my first ship – the F.T. Everard coastal tanker, *Authority*. In between taking the pilots to and from the ships we carried out all manner of duties including the upkeep of the cutters as well as 'housekeeping' in the lodge. Watches were maintained as at sea and we worked two weeks on and two weeks off. The apprenticeships lasted for four years, during which time we were to attend nautical college prior to going to sea as Third Officers. Having obtained a Chief Officers 'ticket' we would then be eligible to join the list of approximately thirty Newport pilots, as and when a vacancy occured. We normally put pilots aboard the inward bound ships at either the Merkur Buoy, about a mile off Barry harbour, or in the case of large ships, near the Breaksea Lightvessel, about three miles out. The pilots would be 'picked out' from outward bound ships from the same positions.

The Bamburgh Shipping Co's, *Longstone*, in Barry Roads at daybreak on Saturday 17 February 1962.

The early weeks of my apprenticeship passed with little incident until mid-February. The authority had been advised that the ore carrier, *Longstone*, which would shortly be arriving from Bona, Algeria, had a seaman aboard who was suspected of having smallpox. As a precaution the pilots and apprentices who would be on duty during the week of her arrival were to be vaccinated against the disease, and the Barry Port Medical Officer attended the lodge to carry out the vaccinations. I was on duty with one of the senior boys on the cutter on the evening of 16 February when, at about 9.00 p.m. we received a call on the radio-telephone from the *Longstone*, giving her position as several miles SW of Hartland Point, and her estimated time of arrival in Barry Roads at 3.00 a.m. The duty pilot was informed who instructed us to request that the *Longstone* should slow down in order to time her arrival off the lightvessel for 8.00 a.m.; he would then board her straight away and take her into Newport on the top of the tide.

I was 'turned in' between midnight and 4.00 a.m. but set off on the cutter in the darkness at 7.00 a.m. As we neared the Breaksea lightvessel we saw the *Longstone's* lights approaching from the westward. The pilot was put aboard just as the dawn was breaking and we returned to Barry. The *Longstone* was moored to buoys in the middle of Newport's South Dock and the Port Medical Officer immediately went aboard. He examined the sick man and diagnosed – chickenpox!

SHIP :- M.V. MOERDIJK

500 TONS GROSS

286 TONS NETT

DRAUGHT :- 8ft 6ins

REGISTERED :- DELFZYL

H.W. 1.18 PM.

Left S. Rock Newport at 10.25 AM (2 Hrs 53 mins to H.W.) At 10.30 AM passed dredger and hopper working at No 5 Bouy. At 10.40 AM. passed the bell bouy and course was then set for Cardiff Roads.

During the course of our apprenticeships we were required to accompany the pilots on trips to and from Newport, and to keep a log of all our journeys. My record of one such trip, aboard the Dutch coaster, *Moerdijk*, is reproduced.

(240° Magnetic to. E.
Cardiff bouy.)

No 1 Sewer bouy aheam
at 10.56.

Aheam of No 2.
Sewer bouy. at 11.11 A.M.
(2 hrs 4 mins to H.W.)

East Cardiff bouy aheam
at 11.22 ($6\frac{1}{4}$ Hrs in 38 Mins)

Passed Rannie bouy.
at 11.50. and aheam of
Sully Island at
12 Noon. Picked out by
cutter 'Spencer' at 12.10 P.M.
(1 Hr 18 Mins to H.W.)

Weather :- Cloudy. light haze
No wind . Sea Calm.

PILOT :-

The English & Welsh Grounds Lightvessel, with Newport visible in the background.

On Friday 8 June 1962 a somewhat unusual boarding broke our normal routine. The Russian steamship, *Myronich*, arrived off Barry on the previous evening and anchored near the Merkur Buoy, where she was due to pick up her pilot on the following morning. As the dawn broke she was seen to weigh anchor and proceed up channel. I ran to the lodge and woke the pilot. He dressed quickly and, still half-asleep, extremely annoyed at having no breakfast, and uttering much invective against 'the Russians', we set off in pursuit. Our radio calls were unanswered, and neither the incessant sounding of our klaxon nor the flashing of our morse lamp was acknowledged. We passed Sully Island, rounded Lavernock Point, passed the Monkstone Beacon and the English & Welsh Grounds Lighvessel before the *Myronich* eventually slowed down as she approached the Newport Deep Buoy, a few miles off the Newport Dock entrance. As we drew alongside and the rope ladder was lowered the pilot came on deck, still uttering less than complimentary remarks about the Soviet Union. Fortunately, the Russian officers appeared to understand little of his colourful colloquialisms and greeted him with broad smiles and a cheery 'Good morning pilot' as he boarded.

Our journey back to Barry was marred by our 'punching' the fast flood tide, and as we had no other ships due for some hours, our coxswain decided that a visit to the English & Welsh Grounds Lightvessel would be in order. We tied up alongside, gave her crew a good supply of newspapers and magazines, and shared cups of coffee and pleasant conversation for a couple of hours, until, with the tide now ebbing, we left and enjoyed a fast run back to Barry.

The pilot returned to the lodge on the following day with the explanation that the master of the *Myronich* was under the impression that he should board the pilot at the Newport Deep Buoy. 'Understandable', said the pilot, with a philosophical acceptance in marked contrast to his attitude of the previous day. His change of heart was, however, explained by his next remark, 'They gave me 400 cigarettes and two bottles of vodka. Not bad chaps, those Russians'!

The pilot cutter *Spencer* in Barry harbour, April 1962.

Friday 29 June was Inspection Day, when the pilots, dock officials and their guests congregated for an inspection of the pilot cutters, followed by lunch at the lodge. In preparation for this annual event an inordinate amount of chipping, varnishing, painting and polishing took place during the preceding weeks. The *Spencer* was the cutter then in use, and no part of her was to be left unattended. Bottom painting (described by one of the senior apprentices as 'a right pantomime!') was accomplished by moving the vessel up the harbour on high water; as the tide went out the sea-legs would be attached to each side, which would hold her upright, high and dry, on the mud. It was then that the apprentices, armed with scrubbing brushes, would move in and set about the removal of the tenacious weed which had accumulated below the waterline. A liberal coating of anti-fouling paint then had to be applied; the whole operation having to be completed within a few hours before the flood tide put an end to the proceedings.

I had been warned that, as the junior boy, it was highly likely that I would be the subject of a practical joke. Despite being on my guard I suspected nothing when I was told by the coxswain to put down my scrubbing brush and go to the stern to perform another task. Only when I was surrounded by my highly amused fellow apprentices did I realise how comical I must have looked, with a small tin of Brasso in one hand, and a rag in the other, polishing the blades of the propeller!

One morning we received a call from the pilot aboard the Blue Funnel liner, *Menestheus*. He had just left Newport and requested that we should leave harbour immediately in order to pick him out a few miles south of the Breaksea Lightvessel – farther out than usual. As we approached the lightvessel we saw the *Menestheus* steaming between the Flat and Steep Holms at considerable speed. We took up our position, and travelling at our full speed, embarked the pilot. 'Why the hurry?', we asked. Her master, wishing to gain the full advantage of the ebb tide, took a middle course down channel and intended steaming 'flat out' in order to reach his next port of call – Liverpool – on the next tide. The photograph above shows the *Menestheus* speeding on her way to the Mersey.

Pilot apprentices at Barry. A 'spoof' photograph inspired by those of the tough, hardy men of the sailing ship days. Back row, left to right, Ronald Boorman, Kent Stephens, and a Bristol pilot apprentice whom I can only remember as 'Ned'. Holding the lifebelt is Alan Thomas and in front is the late John Kirby, who, for reasons unknown to me, was nicknamed 'Tojo'. He was tragically killed in a fire on board his ship some years later.

The *Alpha II* in Barry harbour.

My six months trial period with the Newport pilots ended in July 1962. I had been accepted, and the time came for me to decide whether or not to sign my indentures. I decided not to. For me, like so many sixteen-year-olds at that time, employment opportunities were virtually limitless, and I chose to pursue a career in connection with my other great interest – photography. I felt some regrets at not going to sea and visiting 'foreign parts', but my taste for the salt air was satisfied by regular sailings on the White Funnel steamers; on a more modest scale perhaps, but the Bristol Channel was never dull!

The pages that follow show some of the ships which I photographed from the decks of the pilot cutter.

The Bristol Steam Navigation Co.'s *Pluto*, with a somewhat unusual deck cargo.

The Hain Steamship Co.'s, *Trecarrell*. Edward Hain, of St Ives, Cornwall, bought his first steamship, *Trewidden*, in 1878. All subsequent members of the fleet were given Cornish names beginning with *Tre...* The ships were easily recognised by their black funnels with the large white letter H.

The St Andrew's Shipping Co.'s ore carrier, *Sir Andrew Duncan*.

The Swedish steamship, *Saggat*.

The Irish coaster, *Westcoast*, sets off down the channel, bound for Cork.

Four

Cardiff

Above: The coaster *Willembarendsz* passing Penarth on her way into Cardiff Docks.

Previous page: Ships in the Queen Alexandra Dock, Cardiff, in the winter of 1964/65.

At the close of the eighteenth century Cardiff began its great rise as a coal port. In 1798 the Glamorganshire canal, connecting Cardiff with the coal producing district of Merthyr, was completed by way of a sea lock to the Bristol Channel. It soon proved insufficient to meet the demands of the growing traffic. The increasing volume of trade brought down from the Welsh valleys by the railways had to be met by corresponding dock accommodation. Under the auspices of the Marquis of Bute, Cardiff's first dock, the West Bute, was opened on 19 October 1839. The last of the docks was opened by King Edward VII and Queen Alexandra on 13 July 1907 in the Royal Yacht, *Victoria and Albert*, and was appropriately named the Queen Alexandra Dock. It was the longest masonry dock in the world at the time, capable of accommodating the largest ships afloat. The building of the dock presented many engineering difficulties including the reclamation of 150 acres of land from the sea. The newspapers reported that its opening was 'a colourful and exciting affair with crowds of people including 6,000 invited guests, long lines of bunting, and bands playing. The pleasure steamers were in attendance in Cardiff Roads and even the tugs and dredgers were dressed overall.' Cardiff became the greatest exporting dock in the world and in its record year – 1913 – exported over 13 million tons of coal.

The tug *Royal Rose*, formerly the *Flying Meteor* of the Clyde Shipping Co., awaits her next turn of duty off the Queen Alexandra Dock entrance in 1963. The *Royal Rose* became the *Yewgarth* during the course of that year, under the management of the Rea Towing Co. On 14 September 1965 she sank outside the Queen Alexandra lock while assisting the ore carrier *Aldersgate* to manoeuvre. She was re-floated but broken up shortly afterwards at Cashmore's yard, Newport.

The tug *Westgarth* about to manoeuvre a ship into the Queen Alexandra Dock entrance in 1965. She was sold to Italian buyers in December 1966 and left Cardiff for Naples under her new name of *Serapo*.

Locking out of Cardiff, the F.T. Everard tanker *Aureity*. The Everard company commenced business as shipowners in 1892 with the purchase of a Thames sailing barge. It expanded to become one of the foremost owners of cargo vessels in Great Britain.

The Bristol Steam Navigation Co.'s cargo vessel, *Apollo*, leaving the Queen Alexandra lock.

The William Sloan Co.'s coaster, *Talisker*, in the Queen Alexandra Dock in 1965. The Sloan Co. began operations in 1825 with a fleet of schooners running from Glasgow, through the Forth and Clyde canal, and down the east coast carrying chemicals to London. In 1851 their first steamer joined the fleet and in 1858 the company began its long association with the Bristol Channel. The company became part of the vast Coast Lines group in the late 1950s and the steamships were gradually replaced by motor vessels; the *Talisker*, formerly the *Western Pioneer* of 1955, joining the fleet at about that time.

The Dundee, Perth & London Shipping Co.'s coaster, *Lochee*, leaving her berth in the Queen Alexandra Dock.

The *Bristol Queen* lies at the Pier Head at low tide on an off service day in 1966. The Pier Head was situated at the landward end of the channel known as 'the drain', which led to the entrance to three of Cardiff's docks, the East and West Bute, and the Roath. The *Bristol Queen* sustained extensive paddle damage off Barry, which put her out of commission during August 1967. Both she and the *Cardiff Queen* were broken up in the spring of 1968 after their tragically short lives of just over twenty years.

The *Queen of the Isles* leaving Cardiff in 1968. Following the departure of the paddle steamers, this small motor vessel, built in 1964 by Charles Hill & Sons of Bristol, for the Isles of Scilly Steamship Co., was chartered by P&A Campbell Ltd for a variety of services. She was then sold to the Tonga Shipping Agency, and in December 1970, with additional fuel tanks welded to her deck, left Penzance on her successful crossing of the Atlantic and Pacific Oceans.

High water at the Pier Head. The *Westward Ho* lies at her berth while the *Queen of the Isles* departs on a three day excursion to Penzance and the Isles of Scilly.

The drain also led to three Mountstuart dry docks which, on this occasion, were all occupied. From left to right, the Johnson Warren cargo vessel *Sycamore*, the Strick Line's *Baltistan*, and the Trinity House tender *Argus*.

The Scarweather Lightvessel, having just left dry dock after an overhaul, awaits her return to her station in Swansea Bay. February 1966.

The elegant lines of the former Mersey dredger *Hoyle*, now the sand dredger, *Sand Galore*, are shown to advantage as she approaches Cardiff docks with a cargo of Bristol Channel sand in 1963.

The *Sand Galore* discharging her cargo in the Queen Alexandra Dock. The water spilling over her side is being pumped from the sand as it is conveyed ashore. The *Sand Galore* was broken up at Grimstad, Norway, in the spring of 1966.

The ship ahead of the *Sand Galore* is the *Amicus*, the last of the fleet of the Cardiff company, W.H. Seager. She was sold abroad in the summer of 1963 and renamed *Leela*. W.H. Seager was a native of Ilfracombe who became a ship chandler in Cardiff in 1892 before branching out into ship-owning in 1904. The company ceased trading with the sale of the *Amicus*.

The attractive Finnish steamship *Teti N* discharging her cargo at the east quay of the Queen Alexandra Dock in 1965.

The Norwegian steamship *Hugo Nielsen* awaits her berth at one of the disused coal hoists on the south quay of the Queen Alexandra Dock in 1965. Cardiff had ceased to be a coal exporting port in the previous year.

The Swedish motor vessel *Ivan Gorthon* in the Queen Alexandra Dock in 1965.

The Greek vessel *Agios Therapon* at the east quay in 1968.

The 'counter' stern of the French steamer *Ales*.

The Indian steamship *Jalamohan*, owned by the Scindia Steam Navigation Co. of Bombay, in the Queen Alexandra Dock. The company was established in 1919 and operated regular cargo services between Indian ports and Europe.

Another Scindia steamship, the *Jalamayur* at the east quay.

The Shell tanker *Harpula* being manoeuvred through the Queen Alexandra Dock in 1964.

The Caltex tanker, *Caltex Bangkok*, in the Queen Alexandra Dock.

The Reardon Smith cargo vessel *Atlantic City* laid up in the Queen Alexandra Dock shortly before her sale to Lebanon in the spring of 1963. The Reardon Smith Line was Cardiff's largest shipping company of the inter-war years, nearly all their ships bearing the suffix 'City'. The company had been founded by Capt. William Reardon Smith in 1905 and ceased trading eighty years later.

The John Cory & Sons steamship *Ramillies* in the Queen Alexandra Dock. John Cory was born in Padstow, Cornwall, where he originally owned a number of sailing vessels. He moved to Cardiff in 1872 and by 1900 his sons were operating twenty-three steamers. One of the last steamships owned at Cardiff was the *Ramillies*, owned by Cory's from 1955 to the spring of 1966, when she was 'sold foreign' and renamed *Surma*.

The *Maritimi* in the Queen Alexandra Dock; one of the 2,710 'Liberty Ships' built in American shipyards quickly and cheaply between 1941 and 1945, at a time when U-boats were responsible for heavy losses on the Atlantic convoys. It was said that as long as the Liberty ships made one crossing, they had acheived their purpose. They were of just over 7,000gt and built to a design based on the Sunderland built steamer, *Dorrington Court*, of 1939. Many of them survived the war and operated for many years after.

The Cypriot registered liberty ship *Egnousa* in the Queen Alexandra Dock.

Contrasing funnels. *Above*: The Russian motor vessel *Viljany*, with its hammer and sickle emblem. *Below*: An unidentified tanker.

The iron ore carrier, *Iron Crown*, undergoing maintenance in the Channel Dry Dock.

The Danish motor vessel *Marie Skou* entering the Queen Alexandra Dock.

The Old Passage Severn Ferry Co. Ltd, whose vessels carried passengers and cars across the River Severn between Beachley and Aust, ceased their operations on Thursday 8 September 1966, shortly after HM The Queen had opened the Severn Road Bridge. The company's three ships are seen here laid up in the East Dock, Cardiff, awaiting their fate. They are the *Severn Queen*, of 1934, the *Severn Princess*, of 1959, and, partially visible, the *Severn King*, of 1935. On each crossing, which took between twenty and thirty minutes, depending on the tidal conditions, the vessels could carry an average of sixteen cars, and in their last years ferried approximately 25,000 cars per month.

A corner of the Queen Alexandra Dock in the mid 1960s, showing, from left to right, the Indian motor vessel *State of Kerala*, the mud hopper *Ebbw*, and a part of Cardiff's floating crane.

The bucket dredger *Abertawe* spent most of her career in the port after which she was named, (Swansea), but with the diminishing number of dredgers in South Wales she was occasionally towed to other locations to carry out the vital task of keeping the shipping lanes clear of the Bristol Channel mud. Here she is working in the drain, just off the Pier Head, in the mid 1960s.

With Penarth Head in the distance, the *Abertawe* and her attendant hopper, the *Ebbw*, continue their work while a coaster leaves the Roath Basin.

The dredger *Taff*, built in Paisley in 1946, with hopper *Viscount Churchill*, working outside the Queen Alexandra Dock entrance in 1961.

Five

Newport

Above: Newport's sea-borne trade began on the banks of the River Usk. Minerals and coal were brought down from the Monmouthshire valleys by canal barges and fed into the holds of the waiting ships by way of the riverside tramways. By the early nineteenth century the wharves of the Town Pill, an offshoot of the River Usk, and the river wharves themselves, were proving inadequate for the increasing volume of traffic, and the development of the Newport Docks began. The completion of the Town Dock in 1842 gave a considerable injection to the trade of the port and led to the opening of the Alexandra Dock in 1875 and the South Dock in 1907. The 1,000ft long south lock, situated at the mouth of the River Usk, was opened by Prince Arthur of Connaught in July 1914, and with its width of 100ft, gave access to much larger vessels.

The photograph above, taken in the mid-1960s, shows the Town Reach of the River Usk, looking north-eastward from the George Street road bridge. It shows the derelict remains of just a few of the wooden jetties of the nineteenth century. In the distance can be seen the Town Bridge, with the ruins of the castle beyond. The entrance to the former Town Pill is visible to the left of the bridge, overlooked by the former flour mill. A short distance downstream, on the west bank, the sand dredger, *Camerton*, unloads her cargo at the Moderator Wharf – at that time the only remaining operational wharf on the River, apart from Cashmore's breakers yard, situated out of sight behind the camera.

Previous page: The Newport Screw Towing Co.'s tug, *Dunraven*, astern of the Houlder Bros. cargo vessel, *Swan River*, as she enters the south lock in March 1961.

The British Transport Commission's twin screw, 800hp steam tug, *Gwent*, built at Bristol in 1949, manoeuvring a cargo ship in the South Dock. At the time this photograph was taken, August 1959, the BTC owned a large fleet of tugs based at ports throughout the country. At Newport the BTC's tugs were responsible for the manoeuvring of ships within the dock system and into the locks.

The tug, *Newport*, in the South Dock in August 1959. Built at Northwich in 1956, this single screw, 750hp vessel was the first motor tug in the British Transport Commission's fleet.

Towing the ships out of the locks and into the channel was carried out by the tugs of the Newport Screw Towing Co. Ltd. The company possessed some veteran tugs, a fine example of which was the *Dunraven*, seen here in June 1960, in the North Dock, (the Alexandra Dock of 1875, renamed on the opening of the South Dock). Originally the *Flying Condor*, she had been built in 1914 for service on the River Clyde and arrived at Newport in 1947.

The tugs *Dunfinch* and *Monnow* in the North Dock, in June 1960. The *Dunfinch* was built at South Shields in 1915, and was formerly owned by the British Transport Commission at Hartlepool, with the uninspiring name of *N.E.R. No 3*. She was sold to Haulbowline Industries, Passage West, Cork, for breaking up in June 1961 for £1,700. The *Monnow*, built in 1922, arrived at Newport in 1956. She was formerly owned by the Tyne Improvement Commission with the equally uninspiring name of *T.I.C. Tug No 2*. She was also sold to Haulbowline Industries for breaking up in August 1960.

The *Dunhawk* entering the south lock in March 1961. She had been acquired in the autumn of 1960 from the Clyde Shipping Co. for whom she had been built in 1943 as the *Flying Typhoon*.

The *Dunhawk* in the south lock, March 1961.

Another Clyde tug which journeyed south to the Bristol Channel was the *Battleaxe*, seen in the South Dock shortly after arriving from Glasgow in March 1961, having been purchased from Steel & Bennie.

The *Battleaxe*, now repainted in the Newport Screw Towing Co.'s colours – black funnel with two narrow silver bands – and renamed *Dunfalcon*, in the South Dock, at the end of March 1961. She and the *Dunhawk* were broken up in the winter of 1968/69 and were the last steam tugs owned by the company.

The *Dunraven* and *Dunhawk* assisting a ship into the south lock in March 1961.

The *Dunsnipe* in the South Dock. Built by Richard Dunston of Hessle, she and her sister ship, *Duncurlew*, launched in June 1962, were the first of a new generation of diesel tugs which gradually replaced the ageing steam tugs.

The *Dunraven* laid up in the North Dock, shortly before leaving for Haulbowline Industries breaker's yard at Passage West, Cork, in January 1964.

From the smallest to the largest; the Norwegian bulk carrier *Free State* in the South Dock, June 1960. With her gross tonnage of 19,614 she was, at that time, one of the biggest such vessels to enter Newport Docks.

The ore carrier *Ripon* in the South Dock in 1962. She was one of four sister ships built for bulk carrying for the North Yorkshire Shipping Co. in the mid 1950s, and one of many such vessels built for a specific fifteen year charter by the British Iron & Steel Co. for importing iron ore.

The *Duneagle* assisting the Alfred Holt 'Blue Funnel' liner, *Menestheus*, into the south lock. The Holt ships, most of them named after characters in Greek mythology, were nicknamed 'Blue flues' and their routes took them from the UK and European ports to the far-east.

The Blue Funnel liner, *Lycaon*, in the South Dock. This vessel was one of a small number of Blue Funnel ships which were operated by an associated Dutch company, hence the Dutch flag and her Amsterdam registry.

The *Enecuri* loading coal in the South Dock .The Spanish merchant fleet of the 1960s still included many veteran steamships. This particular vessel, owned by the Compania Naviera Vascongada, dates from 1921.

The Park-type tanker, *Azure Coast*, built during the Second World War, was laid up at Newport, moored to buoys in the South Dock, for about four years before she was eventually sold for scrap. The Dutch, ocean-going salvage tug, *Maas*, is seen alongside her preparing to tow her to the breakers yard at Vigo, Spain, in September 1962.

The Nigerian National Line's steamship, *King Jaja*, built in 1955, and the BTC tug *St Woolos* in the South Dock in the mid 1960s. The British Transport Commission's tugs had, by then, been given a new colour scheme with grey hulls and pale blue funnels with white emblems.

The Kyle Shipping Co.'s *Kylequeen*, dating from 1922, leaving the South Dock with a cargo of coal for Ireland, in October 1961. On the following day she encountered a severe gale off the Pembrokeshire coast, and her steering gear became badly damaged. The Angle Bay lifeboat stood by her and after wallowing helplessly for several hours in heavy seas, the *Kylequeen* was towed by the tugs *Anglegarth* and *Stackgarth* into Milford Haven for repairs.

The F.T. Everard tanker, *Acclivity*, entering the south lock in November 1962. She was a frequent visitor to the South Wales ports and was used principally for replenishing the fuel tanks of oil-burning vessels. She was sold to Belgian shipbreakers in the summer of 1966.

The *Acclivity* refuelling the Silver Line's bulk carrier, *Silvercrag*, in the South Dock in November 1962.

The *San Pawl*, built in 1920, in the South Dock in January 1962. As the former Swedish owned *Burgundia* she was a regular trader to the Bristol Channel.

The British Transport Commission's dock tugs, *Llanwern* and *St Woolos*, alongside the General Steam Navigation Co.'s cargo vessel, *Lapwing*, awaiting the tide for 'locking out' on the evening of Friday 30 June 1961. The *Llanwern*, built by P.K. Harris of Appledore, Devon, was the first twin screw diesel electric tug built for commercial ship handling in the UK, and began service at Newport on 24 June 1960. The *St Woolos*, built by the same company at about the same time, was virtually identical but was diesel engined.

The evening of Friday 30 June 1961 was particularly busy, with the arrival and departure of a large number of ships. All of the channel tugs were fully utilised and the *Llanwern* was required to tow her ship out to sea – a rare occurance for the BTC's Newport tugs.

The *Llanwern*'s ship was the *Swan River*, one of the Houlder Bros fleet of cargo vessels. The company's main routes took their ships between the UK and South America, and the *Swan River* is leaving on the long journey down the South Atlantic to Montevideo, in Uruguay, with a cargo which included a number of single decker buses secured to her deck.

The *Dunheron* outside the south lock. Having just taken a ship out, she is now returning for her next duty. Built in 1923 for the British Transport Commission at Hartlepool, she was originally named *N.E.R No.6*, and was acquired by the Newport Screw Towing Co. in the autumn of 1960.

The *Dunheron* joins the *Dunhawk* in the lock with the next ship to put to sea, the ore carrier, *Longstone*.

The *Dunheron* at the bow of the *Longstone*.

At the end of this bustling activity, the *Bristol Queen* returns from the annual 'Inspection of the Port' charter trip to Ilfracombe by the Newport Harbour Commissioners. This was an event which had taken place annually, except for the war years, since the 1890s, on the last Friday in June. The trip originally began and ended at the Landing Stage on the east bank of the River Usk, just below the Town Bridge, but on the cessation of the White Funnel Fleet's Newport sailings at the end of the 1956 season, and the disposal of the three pontoons to Dutch buyers in May 1957, the passengers embarked and disembarked at either the South Dock or, as on this occasion, the south lock.